Breaking the Map

2009

Blue Begonia Press
Yakima, Washington

BREAKING THE MAP
Kim-An Lieberman

Library of Congress Cataloging-in-Publication Data

Lieberman, Kim-An, 1974-
  Breaking the map / Kim-An Lieberman.
      p. cm.
  ISBN 0-911287-61-2 (pbk. : alk. paper)
  I. Title.

  PS3612.I3346B74 2008
  811'.6--dc22
  2008034292

Printed in the United States of America

Blue Begonia Press
225 S. 15th Avenue
Yakima, WA 98902
(509) 452-9748
bluebegoniapress.com

Trịnh Lệ Sâm

1918 - 2003

CONTENTS

In the Half-Light

Breaking the Map   13
Water Buffalo Tale   14
Invocation   15
Singing the Citadel   16
Down the Dragon   18
Eyes to the Earth   19
The Last Territory   21
Aquarium at Nha Trang   22
Calligraphy   23
Saigon Motorbike Thief   24
Four Folksongs   25
Coda   26

Fifty Different Tulips

Crossing   29
Appleseed   30
Eden Revisited   32
Concerning the Rock Hyrax   33
Prom Night at The Hague   34
Acrobat in Love   35
Achilles on Electric Bass   36
Roadside Bar, Athens   37
True North   39
Mme.   40
The Ritual   41
Second Skin   42
Plastic: A Parable   43
Infatuation Theorem   44
Weekday Exorcism   45
Wings   46
Valediction   48

Learning Their Names

Chuyện Của Bà / My Grandmother's Stories   51
Grandmother Song   53
Translation   54
Assembly Diagram   55
Science Experiment   56
School Choir Trip to Juneau   57
Gingham   59
The Wordsmith's Apprentice   60
Xuân   61
a.k.a.   62
Hearing a Song for the Second Time   63
When Poets Go to the Circus   64
American Daydream   65
Emerging: A Letter   66
Penumbra   67

Weight and Wing

Histories   71
Red River Cathedral   72
Mekong Days   73
Carrying My Dead   74
Icarus Elegy   75
The Untelling   76
Curiosity   77
Memorial   78
Ant Explains Itself   79
How They Built the New Hotel   80
Swallows Nesting   81
Ground Zero   82
Tradewinds   83

Acknowledgments   85
About the Author and the Artist   87
Design Notes   88

To fill a Gap
Insert the Thing that caused it—
Block it up
With Other—and 'twill yawn the more—
You cannot solder an Abyss
With Air.

— Emily Dickinson
546

IN THE HALF-LIGHT

Breaking the Map

They began with a giant carbide ripsaw at the designated parallel.
The course was fibrous and deeply stratified.
The first mile took fifteen days.
Little bits of rock slid from the selvages.
Rivers, disconnected, spurted erratically from both ends.
For railways and telephone lines, specialists were consulted.
Luckily, no mountains.
The project was broadcast live on national radio.
Helicopters buzzed constantly overhead.
Local hardware stores donated tools by the truckload.
Workers hoisted crowbars, jackhammers, pickaxes, grappling hooks.
Entire villages volunteered.
Children distributed free lemonade.
Grandparents stationed lawn chairs on either side.
As the gap unzipped, landowners on the divide had to think fast.
Brothers tossed coins for the better half.
Lovers hopped across together, discarding their old lives.
Airlines held last-minute lotteries.
At the terminus, an official ceremony with golden hammers.
A thunderclap tore through the completed chasm.
Startled, those remaining on the edges waved a mechanical goodbye.

Water Buffalo Tale

Mrs. Willard, expecting catalogs, fainted.
Hearing thuds, Mags & Benno ran to the porch.
Their mother was woozy, breathing damply
in the shade of the beast's ponderous tongue.

Mags & Benno, industrious, mobilized quickly:
three-dollar rides for the neighborhood kids.
In the breakfast nook, icepack pressed to forehead,
an urgent Mrs. dialed Mr. at work.

The backyard flooded with goggle-eyed youngsters.
One boy cried, *Water buffalo—from my country, Vietnam!*
Whatever, Mags & Benno said, *it's ours now.*
The beast shrugged each cheering charge to the ground.

Half-past ten, Mags & Benno dreaming new profit,
Mr. marched out in slippers to untie the beast.
He led it briskly to the far edge of suburbia
where the asphalt faded to ragweed and dirt.

Go on now, urged Mr., *return to your jungle.*
He pushed the bony rump toward a mideastern star.
But the beast stood there stoic, leaning upwind,
returning only a dark glassy blink.

Don't you hear? Mr. yelled, losing his patience,
this is no proper home, this is no proper life!
No answer, no movement: no sudden respect
for kingdom or phylum or season or sense.

So they sat, beast and man, biding the impasse
as stars swiveled tracks through the unanchored night.
The margins of memory dangled around them
like scattered tinsel in the sallow fields.

Invocation

Like the hundred songs that praise
every city in Vietnam
in every season, every age:
Hanoi, you are lost in traffic and karaoke,
are swallowed by the summer monsoon,
are blossoming flames in October.
Hanoi, every day I walk among your
skeletons and burning branches
and every night I sprawl across stones,
dream that I am crawling through
the dust of your explosion,
your black-walled labyrinth,
your rusted gates.

Singing the Citadel

Marketplace

Such mangoes, blushing in lopsided piles,
costly and out of season. Under canvas canopies
vendors crescendo through baskets, pots, crates of greens,
flapping chickens, armfuls of mint, tubs of ginger,
arpeggios of orange, persimmon, pomelo, pear.
Splashing water, small boys run buckets from stall to stall.
A woman in red holds tight the ears of a baying black cow.
Another shakes a string of silver fish. And there, in the corner:
one skinny girl with her mouth wide as a carol
and a cross-legged man, chanting hunger.

Café

Our waitress pours tea for herself and sits beside us,
propping her feet on a chair to keep dry.
The streets burst into sudden rivers, and
still the tempo never slows, save an occasional car
stuck mid-note, its sputtering engine
soaked through. The million bicyclists just roll up
pantcuffs and throw plastic sheets over themselves,
over children perched on the saddlebar, over flowers,
fruits, white geese crammed in wire baskets.
Their makeshift raincoats of assorted pastels
rattle behind like banners on the staccato wind.
A dead rat floats by, one paw curled in a spiral,
and the waitress kicks it away with a lazy heel.

Monument

What is the sound of forgetting?
Shuffling footsteps, idle chatter,
bottlecaps and the fizz of Coke
on a hot afternoon. Long intervals of dirt.
A chorus of grass. One palm tree, light
rushing through holes in the trunk,
and the hush of a hand-printed sign:
"Here is where they shot Mr. X."

Street

Broad-shouldered banyans rise from the sidewalk,
break the moon into coarse white grain.
Rats scuttle under iron fences. Night birds
call in circles. Somewhere close by, a cyclo driver
pedals a beat on his unsteady wheels.
Neither sleep nor day. Neither here nor home.
Counterpoint echoes of silence and sunrise,
a baritone rumble from the gathering monsoon.
Alone in the half-light, I listen for song.

Down the Dragon

Plant your heels firm at China's frayed edges
and ride down the dragon in a swift glide of flame:

down the green swirls of Sapa, indigo Hmong lands,
three-thousand spines shooting through Halong Bay,
salt-spray of Haiphong, deep Red River silt,
Hanoi's cobblestone mazes and ocher facades,

down the narrow throat of the Truong Son Mountains,
stout ribs of Laos, trails graveled with bone,
summer-silk floods in Hue's purple palaces,
Hai Van Pass hidden in hovering clouds,

down the half-vanished scars of Danang and My Lai,
wood pillars of Hoi An, bright sands of Nha Trang,
Cambodia's broad belly, webbed veins of the Mekong,
Saigon's sprawling markets and electric din,

down lotus-leaf pagodas and honeycomb islands,
down verdigris ripples of mangrove and rice-shoot,

to the slim tailtip of Ca Mau, the southern dewclaw,
a blazing descent into sea-scale and smoke.

Eyes to the Earth

Half-breed, they call me.
Only a snip of a dragon, a pinch
of an angel, soft-bellied hound circling
before it squats on scraggly haunches. Only half
my face, half my flesh may call Vietnam
home. The rest, American-imported:
pink flushed hands, hazel eyes.
Half-breed, like oil and vinegar sliding
back to cool separation.

My cousins, scattered by beer-marinated soldiers
in green shoots across the rice paddies,
search. They spread roots
to grip the dust-sown ground.
They spread, path by path, past
Hanoi, past Saigon, hands
dark imprinting the dragon earth.

Cursed before the family
altar where incense spits spires of perfume and smoke.
Thrown into the streets by iron matriarchs,
by sapling girls, with nothing
but dust to whet their stomachs,
dust to water
their tongues, dust
to wear on shivering, scaled backs.
Their scars split skin as pink as mine,
but their silhouettes dig sharp edges in the ground.
Slithering beneath steaming clouds of dirt,
my siblings know their place:
low, eyes to the earth.

I wait, feasting
full on my freedom.
Free I burn between slats of stares,
slurs curling, oblique like sliding steam.
I play their game, writing
exotic scripts and elaborate lies,
writing for tomorrow, for one

dust-child to scratch and slither
down the pavement on bloody, ragged claws, snag
my sleeve and bid me:
Come and embrace all the breathing, breathing dust.

The Last Territory

The dirt, rust-red from yesterday's storm,
lodges thickly in my shoes and fingernails.
Long stems of cactus narrow the walk,
crushed and bleeding a fine, clear milk.
Fields gleam small and dark below.

Overhead, the temple: bleached bricks
patched with lichen, statue of an elephant rubbed
featureless by wind. Broad trees anchored
against undulant sky. I climb up.
A pale sun opens into old walls,
pushing light between wide-cut cracks.

This is a kingdom deep beyond remembrance.
I grasp at remnants of a tired earth—
the wooden bowl emptied of ablution,
household ghosts leering in the leftover rain.

Aquarium at Nha Trang

A round, smooth concrete basin
painted white and filled to the brim:
giant crabs covered in sea-moss,
stingrays, sometimes a dolphin,
three slender reef sharks,
spiraling prisms of fish.
They charge admission,
let you clamber down to the edge
and shake a turtle's leathery fin.
Next door, on the wind-worn dock,
a restaurant where you order lunch
pointing: a net lowers deftly into the pool
for your choice, still shivering saltwater.
At dawn the fishing boats thread back
to fill the sands with black-eyed shrimp,
lobster, jagged knots of seaweed,
retreating again with the tide.
The open water, they say, holds
unimagined creatures. New treasures
like shreds of twisted steel and glass
glinting just beyond the edge of vision.

Calligraphy

This beach, a dappled parchment,
and I stand waist-deep in the South China Sea
under reeling birds and August sky.
Twilight edges the mountains sapphire
and open-sea fishers sail inland to sleep,
their lanterns a necklace strung between rocks.
I stretch my arms into sweeping water
and the tide beats through me.
My most beautiful thing. My ocean.
My boundaries. My edge of the world.
I have come this distance
to see the sun unravel
in strands of orange.
I have come this distance
to know, if it can be known,
what melts into shadow
and what persists.

Saigon Motorbike Thief

In the instant after it happened, as she craned
her neck slow-motion to watch the moped sputter
away she was strangely glad to be free of the chain,
free of the pendulous cross that had swung from her neck—
& even more glad for the extra weight of diamonds
pressed in the gold, extra weight which absent made
her shoulders spring light & tall. Already
the husband was screaming his hoarse-throated scream
spilling gutter obscenities & spitting phlegm at the bright eyes
gathered in unblinking rows not to help but to gawk,
mesmerized by flailing white arms, the magician
who might any moment pull some bunny
dangling by pink ears out of shiny thin air.
She touched a finger to the hollow in her chest
where the cross had kept time like a grandfather clock
& then she touched gently the patch of raw skin
along her shoulder where the chain had chafed & clamped
with jealous teeth before it broke free. Seeing no wizardry
the crowd dispersed to general city mayhem, the husband
cursing one million no-good hoodlums in one fucked-up land
& she wondered: didn't every bright-eyed kid in this town
have a whole mess of crying siblings, greying parents to feed?
What inner engine made one lone boy so brave,
so brave that he could slick back his hair every morning
& ride into the heart of town? Must take some swell ego
to wake the streets, exhaust pipe rattling like a snare drum.
Must be grand to watch the crowds part like the Red Sea
as you zoom across dry & smooth to the other side.

Four Folksongs

—Traditional / Translated from the Vietnamese

Trâu Ơi, Ta Bảo Trâu Này

hey buffalo, say now:
come to the fields, come plow with me
for farming's meant to be
me here, you there, work free as play
when rice stalks bloom away
a grassy harvest waits for you

Mấy Giờ Rồi

what's the time, the drum's not rung
let's head home, fried rice for lunch
troubles fade

Bà Ba Béo

old round Rose
sold pork rolls
seashore store
owed and closed
three, four goes

Qua Cầu Gió Bay

loving, we lose our shirts in the loving
come home, tell dad, tell mom: oh dear
must be those breezes on the bridge
must be those breezes on the bridge

Coda

When the new moon flickers,
I steal a glimpse of Saigon
floating downstream in purple silk,
utterly in love with herself.
Humming the old songs.
Fingers dripping with custard apple,
durian, sticky rice.

FIFTY DIFFERENT TULIPS

Crossing

Perhaps if westward we had scaled
the broad hips of the Cascades,
found resting in the valley a sea
of Douglas fir and bristling pine,
circled our campfires in a place
we named Paradise because the sun
capped the uplands in brilliant gold.

Our own seas were dark, fitful,
torrents of salt that stung the eyes.
We crouched in dim cargo holds
along walls of dank metal
and fish packed in ice chips.
We slept on coils of lanyard,
bodies crammed until no space
remained between dead and dying.

The borders of skin lost meaning.
One child's fever warmed us all
like a spark racing through dry grass.
Although we could not speak
we listened for the sounds of living:
a cough, a stifled sob, a grunt,
the hiss of urine, the rasping hills
of our syncopated breath.

Still in our dreams the endless scrape
of waves across rivets. The journey
ended but we never found land.
We wanted to dig deep underneath,
crush our fingers through the mud
until even our bones smelled of rain.
We wanted to know this place,
cling slow and close as moss
to stone, every season tugging us
back to a common origin.

Appleseed

Born of rib or womb, gender is the oldest art—
maybe the vainest too, cloaking our simpler selves

in amber clouds of powder and perfume,
emerging on stage all mustachioed and muscled.

Call it a nation's adolescent vanity, then,
to refashion her a strange sort of wiry lad—

girl born one crisp autumn, winesap in her cheeks,
gloss of cider-pomace heavy in her hair,

her mother's young grave greening so lush
the neighbors started whispering witchcraft—

or maybe she planted the rumor herself,
forecasting too rough a life for any daughter of Eve

weaned on jonagold juice, fond of lazy afternoons
barefoot among the crickets and garden snakes,

tempted downstream by flickering river-tongues.
And all along the tributaries, a raw trail of truth—

ebony boy John, barely eleven, tutored in steel
by Chinaman Henry, gone in a blast of Sierra rock;

Bunyan's blue-eyed babe, illegitimate niece
with whip-burled back and log-burdened arms;

slender Clem shamed into suicide, miner '49er
caught playing dress-up in his sister's herring-boxes—

everywhere the brown, the queer, the second sex
tightening the ropes on the wagon canvas,

herding the livestock, naming the children,
scrubbing cholera from the threadbare blankets,

digging cemeteries in the dank underbrush,
lips and feet and fingernails caked sepia with clay.

She witnessed, and knew, and bound her sackcloth
tight around the chest and loose on the hips—

learned to walk with a westering swagger,
speak with a bulge of frontier gravel in her throat.

Silenced by the sediment of history, maybe,
helpless to stop the leaf-bud, the pollen, the fruit,

bees abuzz in the blossoms, branches of pigeons
warbling the falsetto of manifest destiny—

but still a thousand buffalo eyes on her russeted ax
chopping down cherry trees by the orchardful,

calling a bitter cultivar to take root, scattering
ink-black pearls of cyanide across the windy plains.

Eden Revisited

Reckless morning glory tangled in tomatoes,
crocus commingled with carrot and wild onions
shooting up despite daffodils. All the labor,
the expert botanists, the hand-lettered placards
gone to waste: years we spent sorting seeds,
learning to tell chives from early cattails, coaxing
ladybugs into lettuce and slugs from strawberries.
Fifty different tulips, set to bud in orderly spectra,
undone by common buttercups. Stray fuchsia,
immoderate orchid. Our rakes stuck in gates of thorn,
we stand empty-handed and watch them arrive:
the new gardeners unfazed by so much chaos,
content with all that beauty out of bounds.

Concerning the Rock Hyrax

Having heard no welcome-word from its closest relative the elephant,
the rock hyrax cancels plans for a cross-savannah vacation and resumes
its usual routine of sunning and snacking on assorted dryland grasses,
dodging wild dogs and cobras, grooming by foot its six sable pounds,
and yes, feeling more than a twinge of self-pity at its lonely lot
as sole torchbearer for order Hyracoidea (not counting tree hyrax,
antisocial sibling, shadily nocturnal, long estranged from the cause).
The rock hyrax spends a housebound holiday papering its igneous walls—
offset lithographs of the dodo, the passenger pigeon, the giant moa—
and faithfully sticking little red pushpins in the Americas map to track,
through news-radio static, one manatee's solo swim up the Hudson,
one more cousin blissfully free of underwhelming girth and inchling legs.
Too soon back to its dreary campaign duty: letters to the editor,
calls to the station, yet another polite but candid way to explain why,
hamster-likeness granted, its heritage spans far beyond middling rodent,
yet another schoolyard presentation charting the extended family tree:
aardvark, rhinoceros, giraffe. Notice the tusks, the rounded toenails
grown iconic on those bumbling kinfolk twice- and thrice-removed,
still patent here in humbler form. The equine gut, the tapir's hind,
even the pachyderm's storied talent to listen acutely and never forget.
How else to explain this bone-deep memory of massive and miniature
strolling together in creature congress, stretching identical limbs,
poking softly whiskered noses into salt-pools at the continent's ebb—
braver beasts wading the glacier melt, roaming the green landbridge,
but all nightly returning to a slumber safe under towering succulents,
to the same rock hyrax dreams, million-mirrored in the Serengeti starlight.

Prom Night at The Hague

Dim gymnasium, floor sectioned and shoe-scuffed,
lone bowl of pink-lemonade punch in the corner.
Crepe paper sloops from the uppermost bleachers.

Australia sways and hums to himself as accordions
wheeze "Waltzing Matilda"; Vienna toetaps the triplets.
Bangkok plucks a spume of baby's breath from her wrist.

Spotlight the Americas in awkward clutch, groping
a smidgen of forbidden culture. Nobody speaks.
Language barriers loom and the acoustics are terrible.

You can tell that Sierra Leone and Peru would prefer
anyplace else, that Sweden just wants a smoke,
that Egypt is fresh heartbroken and single-scene shy.

Stick-on nametags sport a smiling rainbow of icons
and various global niceties: "mahalo!" "ciao!" "très bien!"
Suspenders aflash, the DJ patters blandly between songs.

"Girl from Ipanema" gets some reluctant hips twitching;
Japan leads Latvia into slow and uncertain samba.
It's their party, however flimsy, so why not just pretend?

Fake one night's escape from embargoes, exchange rates.
Ditch diplomacy for two mirrorballs and a rented tux.
Pick any polyester partner. Dance an approximate peace.

Acrobat in Love

When the circus stopped near Fresno for the winter
and her nights were free, she pranced in green sequins
around the old performance hall. Beethoven's Fifth,
her favorite, swept her into C-minor and she somersaulted
over balustrades into the open-mouthed orchestra,
landing with flourish, feet first, on the kettle drums.
Because her body slid through air like a bow, rosin-smooth,
the cellist forgave damage to his A-string. One week later
he pledged eternal love at the Drive-Up Wedding Window
in Vegas. He was skittish, a wiry mop-haired kid
leaning across his father's Plymouth, shy to kiss on cue.

The wedding glimmered in their eyes for weeks.
December and January were cozy, a soft honeymoon
before spring bloomed red tents and popcorn stands.
She hated tightrope a little less with his spotlit smile,
even whistled while toeing the sharp cold wire.
But the life of spectacle gnawed at him, the whole audience
goggling at the prism of his bride's long legs.
She pointed out the safety net and he poked at the holes.
Even the extra cord and harness, her willing concessions,
did not soothe his temper, still left him turning
those triple-flips and arabesques in his sleep.

The finale is always the same for a man who believes
performance is communion, who never dares beyond
second chair. He likely found some Italian villa on the sea,
a place to sigh Chopin under a small trellis of roses.
Or maybe he stopped in Kansas, bought a fiddle
to play the whirling barn dance summer Sundays.
Poised port-de-bras on the platform, she would dream him
a different path every night. She would skip a breath,
grasp his callused fingers, then kick away the trapeze
and draw his name on the warm open air.

Achilles on Electric Bass

Originally it was a gold-studded lyre
or one of those twittering panflutes,
but the year is 2008
and Achilles is no fogey.

So now he sits
high above the Hellespont,
plucking away his warrior heart
on a jet-black '57 Fender.
His square hand
strokes the smooth maple neck.
A little buzz from the portable amp.

With deeper notes, he feels
dull twinges of an ancient grudge—
a girl, a broad-armed boat,
some stolen armor—but then the dust
stirs around his boots.
Swift Aegean breeze. He forgets the rest.

Achilles is man enough
to admit melody's not his thing.
Better to be a timekeeper,
carry the song by its innermost ribs.
One part muscle,
two parts soul.

Roadside Bar, Athens

Can you even imagine? Hours sniffing my way
through total darkness, every corner same as the next.
Walls crumbling into walls, pillars caked with moss.
But you needed no map because you knew the path
by the long sour cut of his bull-breath.
At the clearing, a little table hollowed from stone,
a campfire, a cauldron, a few forks and spoons,
snail shells and coins assembled on the hearth.
Poor kid, just wanted a mother and a good meal,
pronouncing in the saddest voice I ever heard
"Do your worst, I am so tired of pretending"
and bowing his head low as I sliced it off,
the left horn gouging my thigh as it fell to the dirt.
I suppose I could have taken a braver route—
smuggled him out of the palace in a laundry basket,
dug him a secret tunnel, that sort of thing—
but I was a lovesick sap, could only think of Ariadne
cheering my return, admiring my fresh manly wounds
and the head skewered on my sword like souvlaki.
Ari, with her milk-splashed skin and velvet smile,
whispering legends and lore in my ear.
Never did need her silly ball of yarn—
I could smell the clean breeze home like a neon arrow—
all it did was knot and catch around my ankles.
Still let on that she saved me just for the kiss.
In times before, I had brained thick-wit bullies,
strung thugs from trees, served bandits to flesh-starved beasts.
One guy I even stretched in half like a gob of carnival taffy.
But no one warns you, when you bring death invited,
how the dreams descend. I never sleep.
I close my eyes even a second, and I hear that voice
mournful and low in the flickering dark.
"Do your worst, I am so tired of pretending."
Yeah, Ari with those light-up lips, such cliffs I scaled for her.
I remember her sobbing, cursing, as we backed
the boat away from shore and pried her fingers
from the hull. She ran a little way after us,
then stopped slack-jawed in the shoal, the yarn
plaited through her arms like some tattered old garland.

Just as we mounted the beat of the open waves
she lobbed one skein seaward, let it draggle in the tide.
Don't you judge. I had to leave her. Too many memories.
I made my choice to linger in these labyrinths alone—
but damn if I don't still feel the burn of that thread
tugging, tugging me through the lidless days.

True North

Dogs severed the harnesses with their yellow teeth
and single-file darted into the distance.
He did nothing to stop them, glad of motion.
It was pure madness to stare at his shadow
unchanging. He imagined death that way,
one afterimage searing in a hollow skull.
Blankness descending in endless flecks.
A petulant silence. He woke up again and again
blinking in permanent daylight, the sun
also an eye unflinching and revealing nothing.
No starry crest, no sudden merge of latitudes.
Only when the blizzard lifted away in layers
did he start to search beyond the melt.
A thick glass held him, but as he pushed
body entire against it, something began to crack
and with new reverence he realized
that anything was possible: magnets unstuck,
water bursting in shards, the world draped
below him like a hundred blankets of silk.

Mme.

She smells of soil, of moss and snails under a canopy
dripping with mist. Her teeth in front are black
like cinder, her fingers
fat as cigar stubs. With one hand she unfurls
concentric circles in the air. *This,*
this is the widening trail, the knife that burrows through flesh.

The sphere of summoning arms, of expanding ribs.
Of the heart that marches forward, of the lungs that balloon
with excess breath,
when you are listening only to the shimmer of cells
falling, falling in sheets of red down your veins.

She walks clumsily; the weight of her chest bends her cane
in a parenthetical arc. Her toes spiral inward like a dancer's.

Stories are cheap.
You pay, rather, for the long labor of harvest:
for the patina of years spent deep in a pocket, half-forgotten,
rubbed on occasion for good luck. She stares as if through
shaded glass: her eyes are milky blue, lids drooping at angles.

Stories are cheap.
Her voice heaves and ebbs in the thick of a cough.
Blinking slowly, she curls her arms
about her trunk like the tendrils of a fern.

The Ritual

My sister, whose screaming could once splinter lightning,
mutely slipped into a brittle and crystalline sheath.
I squinted and still could not discern the precise moment
of her removal. The strands around her hardened
quick, like burnt sugar on a spoon, and the knocking
echoed sharply in my face.
                              After that, she walked
with a constant glide, as if her feet hooked into hidden wheels.
Even her hands and her hair moved differently, rotating through
a practiced set of motions and returns. I spent many hours
scanning the glossy surface, watching my reflection dip and scatter
at the corners.
                    One still Sunday I pushed my way inside
and waded through the sheets of fog. I found her doubled
on the concrete, various parts curled and glistening like snails.
She rubbed softly in circles, her torso leaving chalky marks
on the wet ground. *How could you?* I screamed. *How dare you?*
But even then, naked and guilty by my direct witness,
she finished the ritual in silence.

Second Skin

Easy to dismiss the first timorous whispers—
all the grandmothers nattering their usual gab,
the children dreaming vague shapes in the fog—

but soon, your own day is a spectrum of noises:
spring-loaded scurry of claws in the rafter beams,
stiff feathers rustling, low grunts from the shadows.

You pretend not to notice, still smiling cordially
at girls tucking thick pink rat-tails into skirtfolds,
old uncles flicking forked lizard-tongues in their tea.

You still nod hello to eagle-beaked neighbors
and stroll casually past the crowd of schoolboys
branching bone-white antlers and leathery horns.

And sundown, alone, after drawing the curtains
and sweeping stray dust from the kitchen floor,
you still tell yourself stories of tethers and cages—

you, with your pale fingers fusing and furring,
awake to the sharpness and scent of the night,
a quickening beat newly barred in your chest.

Plastic: A Parable

In a world of noses discorporate, he plies his craft:
full-service copyeditor, typist, inkfill to the rind.
Daily amendments of the aquiline, the puggish,
the exceptional septum, the flare with too much flair.
Always another in line to be lipoed, lifted, lasered,
drawn in, tuned up, nip/tucked, nine-o-two-one-o'd.

Trained to discern, he grows reflexively disparaging.
Venus atop seashell with slumping, pebbled paunch.
Spider veins cracking across David's marble ankles.
Crow's feet framing Mona Lisa's haggard gaze.
Too late to rescue imprint from its skin-deep mold,
from the dysmorphic droop of artist's palsied clutch.

Beauty taunts him even in the kitchen, summer fruit
overripe with bruises and dimples, juices congealing
as he cuts away and apart what ought to nourish.
A full dozen mangoes discarded in sap-heavy slivers.
Peach or plum or apricot, he pares the flesh to find
only striation in the stem, asymmetry in the stone.

Yet he rejects the fabled easy-out of animated statues,
his own reflection pondside, flickerings in sooty caves.
He learns instead to take idolatry in fractions:
love the half-curve of a shoulder, the eyelid's pie-slice.
One infatuation at a time, this shadow sustains him,
perfecting life in parcels and eclipsing all the rest.

Infatuation Theorem

Star-crossed they were certainly not, but for one moment
suppose: her running monologue with him might echo
his late-night conversations in the pubs of L.A./the Bahamas/Beijing,
those broken-record reveries some slice of the actual tryst
with Ellen/Ling-Ling/Antoinette. Who knows what
he might be wearing these days, or smoking—waiting tables
in a ratty diner, thrusting ice-picks into virgin glaciers.
One more variation and she had lost count. Assume that he still
wet down his stubborn cowlick, still quoted Hendrix incorrectly
and drank his coffee straight. She could glare at that last
black sip for hours, the muddy blots he left on the counter.
But back to the point: there must be a mathematics in it.
If she was not thinking of him 78.5% of the time, surely
the theorem still had room, as he unfolded his morning paper
in charming Toronto/New Jersey/Madrid, to reset all the variables:
that moment, their usual sidewalk, and a crazy purple sunset
crackling before them, torching the roof of the practical world.

Weekday Exorcism

Ceremony in the new millennium seems so superfluous,
gone the way of dinner gloves and Petrarchan sonnets.
When you burn his pictures, you're playing sacrificial music
on high-fidelity CD and sucking up stray ashes with a convenient
cordless DustBuster. All you see in the flame is a shrinking parabola,
Brownian motion, calculable swirl of the known universe.
His face cracks apart like continents separating. Black waves
bury his smile and every other landmark. *Au revoir
demon. I release you. Finit.* You watch the smolder rise and die.

Wings

It had been three years, maybe longer, and the map of his body
    was etched
in her palms. The stretch of his legs. The stiff, clean-shaven line of
    his jaw.
His left ring finger, curved slightly inward. So of course she made
    the discovery.

The first feathers appeared in a pair. She was facing him in the grey
    wash of morning,
stroking the knoll of his shoulder blade, when twin quills broke
    suddenly through the skin.
He locked himself in the bathroom for hours, cursing blankly
    at the mirror.

They grew quickly, eclipsing his back like snowfall. In moonlight they
    were lustrous.
She would brush them gently with a damp washcloth, gather loose
    feathers in a basket.
Under their spreading canopy his muscles formed tight knots, pulsing
    like fists.

He complained about their aching weight, how they poked holes in his
    favorite sweater
and sometimes, of their own accord, began to flap and pull his feet
    from the ground.
Just think of all the usefulness, she said, fan on a flaming night or extra
    warmth in winter.

But he became sullen, took long walks alone after dinner, absolutely
    refused to see a doctor.
He would not go to the beach anymore, even when she promised
    a three-color sunset.
Can't trust these things, he told her, and I'm not stupid. I know
    my mythology.

When he asked her to leave, it was another grey morning. He lay
    sprawled on his stomach
at the opposite end of the bed. He gave no reason, but she knew it was
    another woman

because their beauty was blinding. Even fully clothed he leaked
	gallons of light.

In time she moved on, ripped up his pictures and set the ridiculous
	basket of feathers on fire.
But some mornings she woke drenched in jealousy. Half-believing
	she heard a rustle,
she would stare at her husband's empty back and wonder if anything
	would change.

Valediction

A classic equation: she was loved by one who measured her
as he measured time—in careful scoops, gathered by hand—
but wanted, needed to believe that moments had darker weight.

To mark the months, she drove somewhere still—winter beaches,
late playgrounds, parking lots on the edge—and slept straight
like the hours were white lines on a road. Dreamt of ink, skin.

Her breath slipped out: trails of thought. Oh, the things she
could say in that close, cold space. *You can't keep it caged like a bird.*
Everything shrivels and stiffens and chokes—even the wing, even the bone.

LEARNING THEIR NAMES

Chuyện Của Bà / My Grandmother's Stories

Duckweed

At dawn I crept over my sleeping brothers and ran to the pond. My mother warned me not to play there, but I danced all day around the brilliant edges. A blue-winged bird called me closer and closer, until I slipped and fell in. I was never so scared. I could not swim. Who knows how I scrambled out, but I rushed home from that darkness, silent, curled up on the straw mat and slept. When I woke my mother was cooking dinner. Through the steam she bid me come to her. She touched my hair: it was dry. My face was clean. Then she lifted my shirt and saw duckweed caught in my navel. And she knew I had been to the pond.

Chicken Trick

They sold chickens at the market in large wire baskets. I was only a girl then, but I knew some things. *Come here miss*, they cried. *See how plump this chicken!* And I poked the hen under a wing, as they held it upside-down, and nodded *Yes, yes, I'll buy this one.* When I reached for my money they cried, *Here miss, let me tie the legs for you!* That was how to carry a chicken home, squawking by the legs. But I knew their tricks. I always tied the legs myself. Otherwise they would turn away quick to cut the rope. That plump chicken would get dropped back into the basket and switched for a scrawny one, all bones. They cursed after me, as I walked home with the best hen. *Bet you'll live long, clever girl. Sure you'll live long.*

Firecrackers

My family was never poor, but I liked to have jobs. One morning I went to the firecracker factory and watched the women seal gunpowder in bright paper shapes. *That looks fun,* I said. *Give me something easy to do.* They showed me how to twist petals at the corners, just like a real chrysanthemum. They let me crook the beaks of paper birds that flew away when you lit the fuse. So I worked there, folding pink and yellow triangles, until I got bored. After that I cut lace for French tablecloths. My pockets were always full of coins.

Two-Plank Bridge

Before they thought of cars or trains, men would pull wooden carts through the street, two round poles on their shoulders and passengers behind. Like working beasts, such strong backs. I rode one home, a long trip from town. We came to a small crossing where the bridge was two planks and the geese cackled below. I offered to get down, but the driver vigorously shook his head *no*. So proud. He stepped ahead. Not even a wobble, we tumbled straight into the stream. The man, the cart, the planks, and me. All of us rolling in goose feathers, soaked black with mud.

Red and Gold

I wanted to move to the city, so I opened my own store. Anyone was welcome. I stacked the shelves high with bolts of velvet brocade, sacks of mungbean flour, lacquered wood chairs, even porcelain sinks and bidets for the rich folks. In front was a glass counter full of jewelry, genuine gold. One day I closed my eyes and sifted my hands through the pile. And the ruby ring slipped right onto my finger: I never took it off again. I have lost much in the years, but never this ring. See how it still shines like new. See how it catches the sunlight. Red as the throat of a bird breaking into song.

Grandmother Song

Close as my own face in the mirror, I know
the rippled line of her neck, the rouge granules
dry and lavender-scented in the cup of each cheek,
the reef-knots at each knuckle. She gestures
faintly upward from the bed; I bring my ear
to the rasp of her laboring breath. I watch her draw
pin by pin from the loose chignon, prying apart
its black and silver yarns. I roll the soiled gown
under the clean one, tugging forward on her torso
to prop the pillows underneath. She plucks tiny snaps,
one arm raised, until the high collar and long waist
become a single flap of brocade. The satin pant-legs
slide to a puddle. Underneath is a ruby of blood.
The needles and tubes are webbed like milliner's lace.
Last, the jade necklace, leaking the milk of her heart.

Translation

I take my grandmother to the doctor each weekend.
My Vietnamese is fair enough, the basics at least;
I have to get creative with "hematocrit" and "uterus."
The doctor, pale blue scrubs and a half-smile,
always addresses my grandmother by her first name
though he is 30 years her junior. He briskly nods his head
as I explain, the best I can, each phrase he assigns.
Sometimes he stops me short: *Just translate my words.*
Don't add personal interpretations. Just say what I say.

Appointment over, I take the keys and drive us
home through the usual stretch of street signs.
What's that one, my grandmother asks mile after mile
and, like some proud traffic-law expert, I say:
"Stop," "Yield," "Caution speed bump," "Exit ahead."
But the truth is I have no idea whether my words
connect, if my translations are knowledge or nonsense.
This language engulfs us in separate oceans,
longer and louder than anything I know how to name.

Assembly Diagram

"Gallbladder" is not a very poetic word. Connotes at best
a wormy flailing, something suspect drawn from a viscid pool.
So what do you say? O saver of bile. O cousin to my lungs.
O vestigial hand-me-down from caveman's venison days.
Purse of the appetite. Mother of fret. Root of rancor, impudence, irk.
How to memorialize the queerly repugnant, the primal squish?
Doctors routinely dispatch the pouch, tumid with misshapen pearls
that wink black calcite under the hissing fluorescents. Nothing left
but a recovery without lyric, groggy for weeks in the grey afterward.
You retch from the drugs and feel absurd with each attempt to place
the Rorschach bruise fanning across your half-hitched stomach,
the make/model/year of the divot sunk deep in your ribs.

Science Experiment

I hated learning to spell their names—
paramecium, euglena, amoeba.
These things that throb with life,
shiver thousands of cilia
or wag a whipsmart tail:
why bury them in dead syllables?

And for weeks I was frightened
to drink water, when every drop
held a city.

My margins overflowed:
the regal stentor, mouth singing
a trumpet. The cyclops, gravid
with clusters of eggs. Brittle
diatoms, varied and finespun
as snowflakes.

I gorged them on yeast
dyed Congo red, and thought
my cells are tainted with blood.
I watched them growing,
size always checked by neat
and equal splits of mitosis.
I imagined myself transparent,
dissected by light.

School Choir Trip to Juneau

Not just white, not just drifted
over but utterly blank, vast, absolute.
Trees stud the hillside like traffic cones
halved by shade and darkness.
Walls of snow on either side of the road
taller than me, higher than street signs.
Bare hands along the misted window
clear another dimension of white.

Our robes, voluminous royal blue
trimmed with gold and green satin,
billow across the slippery car lots
where we shake them like kites.
We spill orange juice on the no-stain
Dacron and watch a dozen liquid beads
trickle in stops and jerks down the fold.

Sure there are scandals. Evening dance
inside our host school's gym, flashing lights
and John Kiley with his hand up Erica's shirt.
Sammy resting her head on the shoulder
of some football player from Sitka.
Everyone leans against walls, feigning
warmth in the obvious tundra.

Mostly we stay square and compact.
Standards like "Shenandoah" and "Swing Low,
Sweet Chariot." A Beach Boys tune,
with barbershop flair. One a cappella.
Every hour filtered through warm-up scales,
the metronome of our conductor's hand.
Brace your tongue. Breathe from the feet.

I skip the glacier hike, so tired
of peering over the edge of things.
Just the mundane melt of time
dropping back into its own sediment.
Instead I cash a traveler's check,

buy an overpriced jacket at the mini-mall.
Loud red, shiny. A lucid blot
against this rigid season of sameness.

Gingham

We are children and it is always summer.
Linna, the girl next door, lets us play with her dolls
and braid our hair with her ribbons. Her sister
who is sixteen, quick-tongued and long-legged,
tells us Linna, at two, caught fever and nearly died.
Afterward, her ears still rang and blurred the crisp
sounds that most of us hear. That slow bright smile,
the strange syrup in her speech are the molten parts.
Linna is all the same sunlight to us, pink ribbons
fluttering from our hair and prisms in her window
tossing jots of color across the walls. A sweet summer
and we are always young.
                         Months later (or is it years?)
down the long yellow halls we see Linna (is it Linna?)
huddled over books, creeping toward the exit sign,
her eyes sweeping the path like white beacons.
She does not seem to recognize us, so neither do we
call gaily for her attention, or step ahead to catch
the falling book. She takes a different bus home,
one with wide doors and black seatless gaps, eats lunch
at the table with bent metal legs. Then a new family moves
next door, with an orange-striped cat and flowered curtains
and no kids our age. And then we grow taller, and bathe
ourselves in the bloom, and all the truest things we know
disappear in the shuffle of a million dazzling words.

The Wordsmith's Apprentice

Each day a new lesson. Heating roots yellow-hot.
Vowels blackened in fire-scale. The noun's glassy slag.
I creep underfoot to stir the coals, fill the quenching pail,
watch his hammer strike in the dim forge-light.

Gentler times, he guides my arms into the dance.
Serif clawfoot. Looping cursive row of fleur-de-lys.
Through his grip I feel the raw strength, each new shape
gold-scripted and glowing on the anvil before us both.

I study the scrollwork barred across the windows,
dangling around my neck in dull bronze chains.
Through thick clouds of oxide, I inhale his language,
the dark letters and ligatures iron-branded in my flesh.

I dream bright streams of speech, pure-molten phonemes,
a sonorous heft twisting smoothly in my own two hands.
Unalloyed, I ascend the stage, dripping silver syllables.
A world of word at my lips. The very ore in my veins.

Yet each morning, I awake too slight and too soon,
bedded and bent in the ash of an arsenic alphabet.
At my feet, the slow-burning detritus of dictionaries.
At my throat, an ingot rounding its cool, mute tongue.

Xuân

Swan. Juan. Zoon/Zan/Zun. June. Shoo-in. Exxon. These are all the ways her name is not pronounced.

•

"Ah," says the teacher, with a philanthropic nod, "small world! I once met a man who lost his right foot in jungle combat. And I have a cousin named Sue Ann."

•

Once upon a time, she imagined a best friend named Xavier. They would start a club, taking advantage of all the coolness of X (X-Men, X-ray vision, X marks the spot). They would become great alphabetic snobs. They would build a treehouse with a massive X for a door. There would be a top-secret password containing several Xs. There would be a motto with words like "X-clusive" and "X-travagant." No one else would even dream of joining without proof of a cross-your-heart, birth-certificated X.

•

Once upon a time, her name had belonged to a poet. Barefoot, brilliant, a river of jet-black hair. Dared any scholar in the empire to match her, line for line. Foolish men tried and failed. Professors hid their flushed faces. Mandarins scurried off, silken robes askew. Dozens of wishful boys crowded her doorstep, stammering and blushing and buckling at the knees. She doused them with ice water and sent them home. Wrote five perfect verses for each meek word they attempted. Left an X of wet ink glistening at the bottom of every scroll.

•

Soon, Shane, Sun. X-You-In.

•

X is a buzz. A shock. A shrill stain of dissonance. But also X is a hush. A private breath, a slow melt. The rustle of new leaves. The long bright arc of moon. The silvering start.

a.k.a.

Countdown to parenthood, and I'm obsessed
about the naming. How to sound unique
and meaningful and confident and sweet,
and flow a natural course from first to last,
but not trip teachers' tongues each day in class.
A shield to thwart disastrous puns, defeat
the schoolyard taunt. Not prissy or antique,
not bookmarking some scandal from my past.
The roots of it, dissected and defined,
are useless. Syllables obscure the goal.
How will I answer when you ask "My name:
the origin, the reasoning?" Or stand
to look at you, dear anonym, and know
my choice could never house what you became.

Hearing a Song for the Second Time

Usually you catch a few more lyrics,
tap your fingers and hum a little during the chorus,
realize that "love her" was really "luck hurts."
This moment, right now: a crucial choice.
Either you'll want a third and a fourth listen,
buy the whole album, devour band gossip
and stand in line, amid downpour, for concert tickets—
or flip the radio dial. You think of the lead singer
screaming rabidly at the new drummer (never mind
he's sleeping with her) about the sloppy tempo,
the off-key cymbals, and what's with the look
she keeps giving the guitarist—and everyone else
huddled behind the soundproof studio glass
gritting their teeth. The same stress of perfection:
how to prove you've still got it, haven't sold out,
you're chart-friendly yet slyly intellectual,
you're edgy and modern with a homegrown feel,
you're not too stale, not too experimental,
you're philosophically and emotionally resonant,
you're worth sporting on an overpriced T-shirt.
With only those one, two shots to impress.

When Poets Go to the Circus

Or, more aptly, the sideshow—where we weave our way
through flapping caravans, scribbling furious notes.
A keen crew, we've no need to beat around the proverbial:
we know the real freaks, we know how staring at them
merely returns the tints of our own melancholia.
Here, the Confessional Lyricist In Anguish.
Here, the Man Obsessed With Iambic Tetrameter.
Why here, then, at all? Mainly for the cotton candy,
melting metaphorically on the tip of the tongue.
Also the elephants, whom we pity for their preposterous nostrils
and the pastel skirts rigged around their hips.

American Daydream

Long afternoons I coast down Far Hills
past the strip malls, the new Borders,
the chunky warehouse stores with SuperSale signs.
It's never clear to me where the suburbs end
and the city begins, just red-trim housing complexes
with clipped lawns rolling one into another,
districts with sturdy names: Oakwood, Kettering,
Centerville. The sidewalks are clean and empty.

When I get home Mike from next door is in his garage
fixing his car again, adjusting the brakepads this time.
He tells me how he squealed past the lawyer's place
late 'ast night to piss him off, cranked up his six-foot
Powerbass speakers and blasted Air Supply.
It's been war ever since that lawyer moved in last month.
Not much to do here, he says, wiping the grease
on his pants. Not much to do but sit back,
sip a beer, watch Oprah, mess with the rich guys.
His Chevy glints bottle-blue in the sun.

Emerging: A Letter

So I tell you, when I came back to start the new year
all of them stared at me like I'd emerged from the jungle,
the prison camp, the dark side of the moon,
      the war zone, they meant, but that's so impolite,
and they asked gingerly *how was it?* and I stared back
with a smile and mumbled *fine* because face it, they didn't want
any other answer.
      It's not over yet. It's still going. It's sounding the hours.
I snapped awake and found myself on an unswept floor,
legs tightly crossed, sobbing. I pushed through layers of white
wet and thick against my lips. I reached the surface
and swallowed too much air.
      You'll never be the same again.
The night before I left, you cornered me in the elevator
and told me a secret. *Things are changing,* you said,
unprecedented things. The floors ticked past.
I laughed out loud. What's the surprise?
We always knew that I would leave and you,
stubborn friend, are stuck in transit.

Penumbra

Passing midnight, the city shuts down.
Streetlights frame the avenue in angles
grey and dim. A regular drip of water
parses time on concrete: here, here,
I am here. We lie stretched long
on the cool hard rooftop, scanning
the sky like a cipher.

A thread of white light hems
the moon. You say stars are territorial:
they carve a thousand tracks
yoked to the mute round north.
This is why you ignore maps,
arrows, stop signs.

I know you are already lost.
But a full-skirted moon drapes
the horizon, edge to edge.
I turn toward you, my familiar path,
and pretend not to feel
my own revolutions.

WEIGHT AND WING

Histories

A year, a decade, a lifetime—and now the fields
ripple golden in the open sun. Daybreak to dusk,
every boulevard ripe with the song and smell of traffic.
New buildings, majestic, stretching city across cloud.

Each lucent morning, tourists alight with regular ease,
meander through the marketplace, take tea on the lanai.
They stand smiling at the feet of marble monuments,
prop an arm on the plaque, start their flashbulbs sparkling.

Always, we have discovered death alongside beauty.
Poppies sprout wild red in the trenches, thousand-fold,
float an opiate syrup across the graveyard gates.
Above saints' skulls, cathedrals spire toward heaven.

No different in this harbor, however calm and blue.
We know what sustains the sweet veneer of time.
Under every gleaming flagstone, a broken body.
Dry bones rattling their histories in the garden bed.

Red River Cathedral

One man and his god against the alluvial shift.
He drives bamboo stakes into a dozen silted acres,
points bloody palms at the four corners of the nave.
Drags whole ironwood trees through the paddies
to make a dense thicket of pillars, spans them with
granite slabs. Twenty more tons to plot the altar,
the stout parapets, the tilting terracotta roof.

Such weight for a muddy land. These crude shores
shudder at the touch, fold with the river's yearly rise.
Yet a marble madonna bears unbroken witness
as nuns drone their vespers in heavy grey wool.
And later, when loud war wreaks its own miracles,
luck means gleaning wisdom from that leaden faith—
conjure a stone's gaze for monks saffron with kerosene,
for women and livestock piled three-deep in the ditch.

So too when my grandmother arrives in California
clutching a rubble of cheap fabric scraps, her tongue
numb to any new language. When her older sister,
Canada snowbound, oils onto canvas after canvas
all tints of northern earth and stoically awaits news
from a son who boarded a long-ago boat, who promised
to shelter his wife and children from the swollen salt.

So too when I arrive, light-eyed for my birthright,
to marvel at this dark cross still carved into the delta.
When I run my fingers along the chiseled fretwork,
the bas-relief angels, the boulder-battened walls.
When I reach the churchyard beggars and go silent,
push alms into the mire of hands, try hard to believe
that one must keep sinking for the other to be saved.

Mekong Days

Tell me a story about the river.
It's not a gentle river. It will keep you awake.
Tell me anyway.
Close your eyes.

•

The surface is a heavy brown
sputtering mud, brewing storm.
Along the edge the current grinds
its snapping teeth on soil
and tree roots, exposed, seize empty air.
From the far bank, someone yells.
You freeze mid-breath in the thatch.

•

Remember how we slept in the reeds?
The safest bed we knew.
I bet we looked silly from above. Half-swallowed.
Let me finish the story.

•

Soon you walk a constant puddle.
You learn the rise and ebb of fever,
the fluid tide of escape.
You wade through bodies and oars.
Somewhere downstream, the salty mouth
spews forth an ocean. Another life
or a second drifting death.

•

Why did we trust it so long?
The river carves the land. The river feeds the fields.
But the flood came, and we lost everything.
Still the river guides us home.

Carrying My Dead

Their legs are stiff and kick
at my hips as I walk.
Every morning I am hungry
from the labor.

We gossip to fill the lingering
miles. I tell them of people
I knew, faded in the tall fog
of city cubicles.

Under my feet the skeletons
of an old flood: prickly leaves,
the hard shells of locusts
gorged to death.

At night I build a fire
and lay their heads near mine.
I sleep, and wake, in the coiling
cold of their hands.

Icarus Elegy

my husband coached him, launched him from the cliff
but I was the one keeping watch as he fell

useless bickering that it is your fault, my fault,
the epic stretch of retrospect blurring what is true

and every night I see him plunge on the TV news,
his breaking body splayed across the front page of the Times

the ocean is a graveyard of splintered boys,
I dig my fingers into the sand and grasp the tip of a feather

why should I care that others have flown higher?
who gains from loss? what progress are we making?

they say it is women's work, this endless weaving,
that we craft the finer seams, the tighter cloth

to spread across the chasm, to quilt the hard earth,
to catch these daughters and sons raining from the skies

but I cannot leave the land of men, their sirens and torchlights
and my child, my child ever sinking in the cold black sea

The Untelling

Triumph: always the start.
Golden fanfare, a hundred festooned footmen waving banners.
Spun-sugar lilacs and doves. Confetti.

Next the great revelation, the evil stepmother's scene.
She rises from her deathbed fairer than ever.
The dagger drops from the dragon's neck. The wound knits itself shut.

Rose-briar thickets wither into soil.
Castles unbuild, rough-hewn stones clogging the mossy moat.
Silence at the abandoned loom, the half-tilled garden.

Somewhere, a knight discharges his hapless squire.
Magic boxes slam. Birds turned human become, once again, birds.
Wolves reclaim the path.

A girl, glass-shod, unfolds her blanket in the ashes.
A boy on horseback retreats trembling from the dark wood,
leaving enchantment to its own devices.

Curiosity

When they killed the cat, the whole neighborhood
gathered around the small headstone
and placed flowers, pebbles, fallen feathers,
pennies—whatever seemed proper
or whatever could be fished from pockets.
A lanky boy stepped onto a bench, eulogy prepared,
but the paper crinkled in his nervous hands
and was hard to read in the rain.

Eventually the neighbors dispersed, each to his own
lowly hearth. Their tracks didn't stay long
in the deepening mud. As they trudged home
shrugging off drizzle, they murmured
about the lonely hill and bench, still
pocked with the soggy footprints
of the lanky boy whose voice had faltered.

But the boy, who stayed behind, tells me other things.
When the voices faded under the drip
of water from leaf to ground, a dozen flames
snapped awake among the weeds.
All the strays, ragged coats of marmalade,
slinking through the mud.
They lapped with silent tongues
from the water pooled under the stone,
strange greed in their moon-green eyes.

Memorial

You miss her, this friend, in proportion—
long enough to offer a standard condolence
as you shake hands with her two solemn sons.
Well enough to nod your head sincerely
when someone speaks of abiding faith,
the fragile heft of life, the slow peace.
The day she started wearing her headscarf again,
elegant, like a bridal veil. The day she drove
around the block and gently handed
each of her houseplants to a different neighbor
with instruction cards for their water and care.
The day when, seeing lunch-guests to the door, she
doubled to the carpet like a branch struck
by a swift breeze. And then, unblinking, rose up
to finish the farewell. On the table, near flowers,
her wedding album—huge kodachrome plates
glowing sepia and olive with their age,
the groom barely out of high school,
the bridesmaids swathed in smooth pink tulle,
pillbox hats to match. They're all beaming
as she stands center in white kid gloves
and squares the camera with a crooked smile.
You know her, the girl posing for the storybook,
only by the dimmest outline—and by that smile.
All the gaps, the histories you never heard,
are etched there in that slice of time
like some coy secret hovering on her lips.

Ant Explains Itself

a kinetic hunger, a quivering fuse,

perpetual progress, joyous tremble, horizon unzipping forth,

the distant sugar of home, of certain returning, but still always hunger to
prod and stretch and burn,

the bitter trek-bound language,

all fancy footwork, loopings and curlings, prisms, permutations, vast
expanse of floor-wall-ceiling, of tree-root-ground, giddy dark brink
of the wandering void,

sweet crush of brother's scent, of cousin's corpse, the cloying imperative
to follow and find and carry away,

to trust the warm waxen chambers, the good glory within, the truest
commands and most sacred edicts, whispering knowledge of
where, of why,

to scrabble, to zigzag,

to be maimed, drowned, flattened, buried, trapped, inhaled, desiccated,
lost, forgotten,

to taste a crumb and not know the bread from the poison,

to feel the wrap of web, the cradling chill, eight spindles shaking down
the gossamer string,

oh smallness pinned with such purpose, such infinite energies,

to revel in each bright inch, each speckled step, each bit of destiny for the
ones who come next, and next

How They Built the New Hotel

Just before sunrise the men would return.
Squatting in rubber thongs, shirtless,
they balanced on the roof—slowly becoming
a floor—littered with rocks and rusty scraps.
Even with my window shut, the constant clink of
metal on metal, steady sawing pried me awake.

A crew of boys, sweaty and interchangeable,
dashed slipshod up a rickety ladder, hugging
jagged bundles of plywood and recycled nails.
They lifted heavier things—bricks, cement—
using a white bucket rigged with pulley and rope.

Untrimmed tree branches, stubbornly clutching
those last snips of green, jutted into gables
and balconies-to-be. All odd angles and dust,
the building seemed not new but decaying,
gaping dumb and eyeless as a gutted crater.

I watched them lay brick, eat lunch, piss,
sometimes yell down for a hammer. Not until
nightfall, when the boys scurried home
in the lamplight, did the men—carefully, tiredly—
descend. Their leaving brought a giant silence.

Once a man glanced across the alley and saw me
seeing him. He stared blankly for a minute,
then resumed his task and never looked up again.
Most didn't notice, though, how I proctored
this daily progress—or if so kept oblivious,
sensing my deep irrelevance to the work ahead.

Swallows Nesting

That spring, as I hauled boxes into the new house,
a pair of swallows started building their nest
at the entryway tucked just beneath the eaves.
A fascination at first, watching their erratic swoop
toward the trees and then the quick veering
back with beaks full of scraggy twig. They played, too,
around and around the clear pond next door,
shimming their stomachs along the surface.

Coming home at night, I would glance up
and see them perched smugly in the overhang,
flanking the near-finished nest and plainly ignoring
my regular traffic. Good neighbors enough.
But then droppings began to splatter the windows,
the welcome mat. My first houseguest assaulted
by a volley of indignant screeching. Half a cookie
pecked to crumbs, as the grocery bags rested
just a few short minutes on the doorstep.

Finally, splotches of white on my favorite shoes.
I knocked down the nest with a garden rake,
muttering under my breath. The birds darted out
squalling alarms, flapping an elliptical patrol
but gradually realizing they had no fort to defend.
For a time, they hovered, with intermittent prattling.
Then wingbeats, then silence, and I was alone.

In the morning, grown remorseful for my victory,
I hammered wooden boxes into nearby trees
as peace offering. But the swallows did not return
that spring, or the next. My living continued,
a parade of empty houses and uncharted cities,
each time the landscape rebuilding itself around me.
In the calmer years I wonder after them,
my fork-tails, my rudders in the turning wind.

Ground Zero

We are irredeemably awkward: clunky appendages,
misplaced hinges, groping gait. We cannot shrug
this human mold with its gravity, its sagginess,
thighs apelike but unsure to mount the canopy,
arms avian without the crowning of plumes.
Throttled, we nurse a fascination with flight:
brilliant buildings erupting upward, bridges
yawning past every divide. We fly into love,
inches above earth. We fly into billowy gowns,
eiderdown duvets, cameras chasing the ball
launched over and out of the awestruck park.

The lift-off from ground zero is such small surprise
that businessmen, ties flapping in the airstream,
and girls whose skirt-hems dance around their ears
rate just one quick blip on the evening news.
Funny how well we know the path, the pitch
of that unchecked chute across the stock-still blue.
How we dream ourselves, tiptoe on the open ledge,
making perfect counterpoise of weight and wing:
one calling its elements back to the core, the other
surging sure and skyward to a higher kind of grace.

Tradewinds

Streaks of cloud clutch the engine.
The land below is cut with rivers,
a glimmering reach of marble and mud.
You are flying alone. Against the spin
of the ordinal world, your minutes
collapse in the glassy backdrop.
One burst of light. One itinerant star
tracing circles in your wake.

The skyline is an inverse ocean,
lazuline mountains spilling water
and ice into the concrete clouds.
The waves are rippling landscapes,
long concavities of ebb and flow,
delicate fractals of grass and pebble
pressed in the tides. The rain quickens,
and you cup your hands to catch.

Soon the travel has seeped past
your skin, arms an hour apart
from fingers, the rhythm of breath
reset. You stretch the distance,
counting shadows that creep down
corrugate walls. Days open and pass.
The decision remains suspended,
pure and weightless and mute.

Destinations bloom dark and soft,
like violets. You skim their borders.
The windows give little blinks:
hazy embankments, rising mist.
You have no guidebook, no map.
No matter. Perhaps now you are ready
to inhabit the risk of never landing,
find home in this anchorless space.

Acknowledgments

The editors and staff of the following journals graciously gave a first home to some of the poems appearing in this book.

Asian Pacific American Journal: "Invocation" and "Crossing"
CALYX, A Journal of Art and Literature by Women: "Translation"
Dayton Voice: "Eyes to the Earth"
Poetry Northwest: "Water Buffalo Tale"
Prairie Schooner: "Wings"
Quarterly West: "Saigon Motorbike Thief" and "Science Experiment"
Threepenny Review: "Mme."
UNM Honors Review: "Eyes to the Earth"
ZYZZYVA: "Eden Revisited"

•

"Four Folksongs" represents original English-language translation from traditional Vietnamese *ca dao* (oral folk poetry), children's chants, and song lyrics.

•

My first thanks to Terry Martin and Jim Bodeen for believing in my words, to Karen Bodeen and Misha Zadeh for turning those words into pages, and to Sam Green for showing me where to start.

My deepest gratitude to the many teachers and mentors who have guided me through the years, especially Jim Clowes and Darlene Sherrick, and to the good friends who have grown with me along the way.

My love to my family, near and far.

Most of all to Matthew, who writes the best rejection letters, and to Cassia and Kellan, who make everything else possible.

About the Author

Kim-An Lieberman was born in Rhode Island and raised in the Pacific Northwest. She holds a Ph.D. in English, specializing in Vietnamese American literature, from the University of California-Berkeley. Her poems and essays have appeared in *Poetry Northwest, Prairie Schooner, Quarterly West, ZYZZYVA, CALYX, Threepenny Review*, and the anthology *AsianAmerica. Net: Ethnicity, Nationalism, and Cyberspace.* Currently a faculty member at Lakeside School, she has taught writing and liberal arts in a variety of settings, from 5th grade through college. She lives in Seattle with her husband and two children.

About the Artist

Misha Zadeh was born in Tehran, Iran and grew up in suburban Seattle. A graduate of the University of Washington Visual Communication program, she worked at several award-winning design firms before starting the company Turquoise Creative in 2001. Her own line of stationery, featuring hand-cut paper collage and letterpress illustrations, retails nationwide and has been reproduced by Chronicle Books, Tiny Prints, and Madison Park Greetings. Her design work has been recognized in *Graphis, Print, Typography, Sunset Magazine*, and *O: The Oprah Magazine*. She and her husband have two young sons.

Design Notes

The cover of this book was designed by Misha Zadeh, with textures and colors digitally sampled from Southeast Asian papers. The sky and blue circle feature a traditional Vietnamese woodprinting paper handcrafted from tree bark, seashell powder, and sticky-rice paste. The red-orange bird is rendered in a contemporary mulberry-lace paper from Thailand. All of the bird silhouettes are the artist's original illustrations, after a photograph taken during her travels in Paris.

The text was set by Karen Bodeen in Minion Pro, a classic font inspired by Europe's Late Renaissance typefaces and inclusive of Vietnamese diacritics. The cover and the section dividers also make use of Myriad, a sans-serif cousin to Minion. Both fonts were created by Adobe Systems.